You Are a Garter Snake!

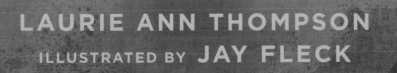

LAURIE ANN THOMPSON

ILLUSTRATED BY JAY FLECK

DIAL BOOKS FOR YOUNG READERS

You are a garter snake!

You have just been born.

You **PUSH**

and **POKE** at your birth sac.

At last, you break free and

BREATHE

your first breath.

Your mother is nearby,
but you and your siblings are
ready to live on your own.

You

STRETCH,

then

SLITHER

slowly across the grass.

SLITHER!

STRETCH!

Your skin feels too tight.

You

RUB

your nose
against a stone.

You

BEND

your body around
a branch.

You
SHED
your old skin.

Yes, that feels better!

RUB!

BEND!

SHED!

Now it's time to hunt.

You

FLICK

your tongue to sniff the air.

You

CRANE

your neck so you
can see better.

Something moves . . .

FLICK!

CRANE!

PEER!

You

PEER

through the reeds.

A worm!

You

STRIKE.

The sides of your jaws

BITE

to **HAUL** the worm in whole.

You **SWALLOW.**

Yum!

After a nice meal, you want to
REST.

You
WRIGGLE
onto a rock and

BASK

in the sun.

Watch out!
That turtle looks hungry.

REST!

WRIGGLE!

BASK!

The days get shorter and colder.
You need to find a den for the winter,
but it is getting harder to move.

You

CREEP.

You

CRAWL.

You find many snakes outside
a hole in the ground.

You all **SLIDE** inside,

COIL

into a cozy spot,

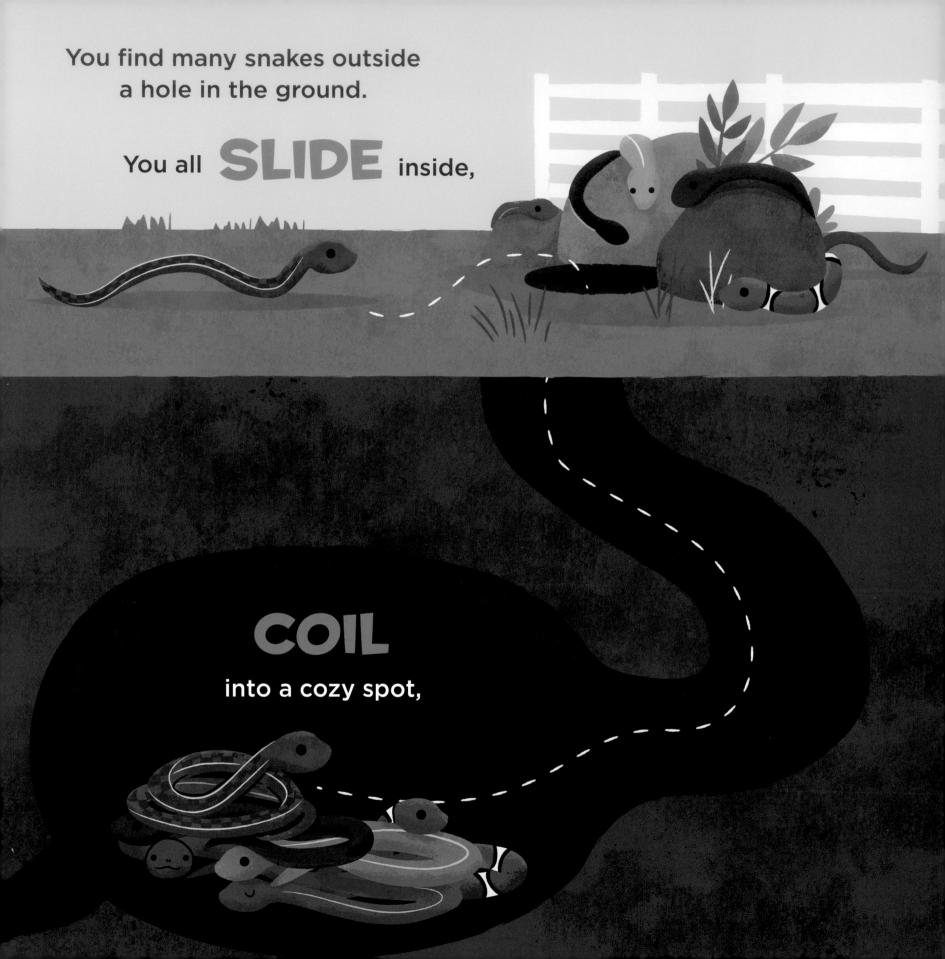

and
REST.

SLIDE!

COIL!

REST!

Sometimes you get too cold, so you

SQUEEZE

down deeper in the den.

When you feel warm, you

SQUIRM

back up.

On warmer days,
you come right out and

SLUMBER

in the sun.

SQUEEZE!

SQUIRM!

SLUMBER!

Finally, it is spring.

You **SLIP** out of the den.

You **DIP** your mouth into a puddle.

You

SIP

up drink after
drink of water.

Ah!

You're ready to go
back to your pond.

It's good to be home.
But one day, you see
a shadow.

A hawk!

You

FREEZE.

You

FLATTEN.

You
FLAIL
as it grabs you
and flies away!

You

SPRAY

smelly, slippery musk from
a gland near your tail.

You

TWIST

your body this way
and that.

It works!
The hawk drops you.

You
HIDE
in the tall grass.

You are safe once more.

SPRAY!

TWIST!

HIDE!

Every day, you

STALK

through the grass,
hunting for slugs.

You

SNEAK

through the reeds,
hunting for frogs.

You

SWIM

through the water,
hunting for fish.

You eat, you grow, you shed—
over and over again—because you are a

garter snake!

Fun Facts About Garter Snakes:

Garter snakes can be found across most of North America, even in big cities. Have you ever seen one?

Baby garter snakes take care of themselves from the moment they are born—without any help from their parents!

Snakes don't have ears, but they do have bones inside their heads that sense vibrations in the ground. This is similar to the way people hear by feeling vibrations in the air.

Snakes use their tongues for smelling! When a snake flicks out its tongue, it picks up scents from the air. Then it presses its tongue against a special organ in the roof of its mouth to sort out the odors.

Garter snakes have four rows of teeth, but they don't chew their food! Instead, the sides of their jaws work one at a time to pull food into their throats until they can swallow it.

Snakes need water, but they don't drink like people. A snake's lower jaw acts like a sponge, "soaking up" water so the snake can drink.

Snakes, like other reptiles, can't create much of their own body heat. Their bodies are the same temperature as the air and ground around them. They do like to be warm, though, which is why they spend so much time basking in the sun.

Garter snakes may keep growing their whole lives! Experts can count the rings on the tailbone of a garter snake's skeleton to tell how old it was. They can live up to around twenty years.

A garter snake may travel as far as twenty miles to reach its winter home, which may be inside an old animal den, anthill, tree stump, rock pile, or small cave.

In Manitoba, Canada, around 15,000 garter snakes spend each winter inside a limestone cavern about the size of a living room. In the spring, they all come out around the same time. Can you imagine?

Glossary:

BASK: To relax and warm one's body

BIRTH SAC: A clear, thin bag surrounding a garter snake at birth

MUSK: A smelly liquid made by some animals

SHED: To lose or take off a natural covering, such as skin or fur

Be a Garter Snake!

Lie down on your belly and try to move without using any other part of your body. Can you slither like a snake?

Spread your fingers out in front of your face like stalks of grass. Now crane your neck, peer though the "grass," and flick your tongue. Is there any food?

Find a comfortable spot in the sunshine and bask for a bit. Humans like it too!

Next time you get undressed for bedtime or a bath, pretend you are shedding off your too-tight skin. Doesn't that feel better?

Slide into bed, curl your body up into a ball, and enjoy a nice long nap. Zzzzz . . .

Why Garter Snakes Are Important:

Garter snakes—sometimes called garden snakes—are good for gardens, since they eat many kinds of animals and insects that eat plants. Seeing a garter snake in the garden means there will be more food and flowers for people to enjoy.

Garter snakes are also food for many animals in the wild, including birds, fish, turtles, raccoons, weasels, and even other snakes.

Just like honey bees, raccoons, robins, and other wild animals, garter snakes are a natural and needed part of the world we all share.

How to Help Garter Snakes:

Keep pet cats indoors. They may hurt or kill garter snakes.

Do not try to touch or pick up a garter snake without help, and never keep one as a pet. Garter snakes are unlikely to hurt you, but you could easily harm them by accident.

Garter snakes often live near water, so help protect and restore wetlands. Keep streets clean so only stormwater goes down drains. Don't mow grass growing near water—snakes might be hiding in it!

FOR DREW —L.A.T.   **TO AUDREY —J.F.**

With special thanks to Dr. Amanda Sparkman at Westmont College

Dial Books for Young Readers
An imprint of Penguin Random House LLC, New York

First published in the United States of America by Dial Books for Young Readers, an imprint of Penguin Random House LLC, 2024
Text copyright © 2024 by Laurie Ann Thompson • Illustrations copyright © 2024 by Jay Fleck

Dial & colophon are registered trademarks of Penguin Random House LLC. The Penguin colophon is a registered trademark of Penguin Books Limited.
Visit us online at PenguinRandomHouse.com.
Library of Congress Cataloging-in-Publication Data is available.
Manufactured in China • ISBN 9780593529782
1 3 5 7 9 10 8 6 4 2
TOPL

Design by Sylvia Bi • Text set in Gotham • The illustrations were created digitally.